Gardening

Patio Gardens

Lori Kinstad Pupeza

ABDO Publishing Company

visit us at
www.abdopub.com

Published by ABDO Publishing Company, 4940 Viking Drive, Edina, Minnesota 55435.
Copyright © 2002 by Abdo Consulting Group, Inc. International copyrights reserved in all countries. No part of this book may be reproduced in any form without written permission from the publisher.
Printed in the United States.

Photo credits: Corbis, Corel
Contributing editors: Bob Italia, Tamara L. Britton, Kate A. Furlong, Kristin Van Cleaf
Book design and graphics: Neil Klinepier

Library of Congress Cataloging-in-Publication Data

Pupeza, Lori Kinstad.
    Patio gardens / Lori Kinstad Pupeza.
      p.   cm. -- (Gardening)
    Includes index.
    Summary: Provides instructions for growing plants in containers, including how to create a flower-filled pot for your balcony and a window box with fruits and vegetables.
    ISBN 1-57765-034-4
    1. Patio gardening--Juvenile literature. 2. Container gardening--Juvenile literature. [1. Patio gardening. 2. Container gardening. 3. Gardening.] I. Title. II. Series: Pupeza, Lori Kinstad. Gardening.
SB473.2.P87   2000
635.9'86--DC21   98-11987
                            CIP
                            AC

Dial Before You Dig
Before digging in your yard with a motorized tiller, call your local utility company to determine the location of underground utility lines.

Contents

Getting Started

In a patio garden, plants grow in containers instead of the ground. This allows you to have a big garden in a small space. So patio gardens are a good idea if you live in an apartment or have a small yard.

To begin your patio garden, you will need to pick a good spot. You can put big, flower-filled pots on your front steps or balcony. Or, you can fill window boxes with your favorite vegetables. The options for a patio garden are endless!

Once you decide on plants and containers, it's time to gather your supplies and plant your garden. As your plants grow, remember to **fertilize**, weed, and water them. Soon, your containers will brim with colorful flowers or hearty vegetables!

Gardening Tools

Turning Soil & Weeding

Hoe

Raking

Garden Rake

Watering

Watering Can

Hose

Planting

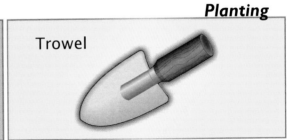

Trowel

Digging

Shovel

Spading Fork

Pest Control

Sprayer

The Right Spot

The first step in creating a patio garden is deciding where to place the containers. Do you have a sunny spot on a balcony? Is the front step shady? Is one side of your house sunnier than the others?

An area that gets sun for most of the day is a good spot for a patio garden. If you have only shade, that's okay, too. Some plants like only shade.

The spot you choose should also be sheltered from the wind. This will prevent strong winds from blowing over your pots. Plants also grow better if they aren't being blown sideways.

If you don't have space for big pots, that's fine. You can use hanging baskets instead. Window boxes also work well if you have limited space.

4171

Your front steps are a great spot to begin a patio garden!

Making Plans

Once you've chosen a place for your patio garden, you can begin planning how it will look. Do you want to grow big, bright flowers? Or, would you rather grow fresh fruits, vegetables, or herbs?

Knowing the amount of sun and shade your garden will receive can help you plan what to plant. Fruits and vegetables grow best in areas that get sun most of the day. If the area you picked is shady, you will need to pick flowers that grow well in shade.

When planning, it is also important to consider your climate. A frost zone map shows your climate's last frost date. Knowing the last frost date in your area will help you plan when to plant your garden.

Frost Zones

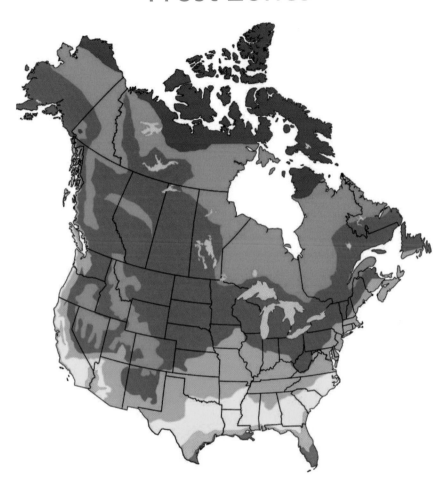

Date of Last Frost

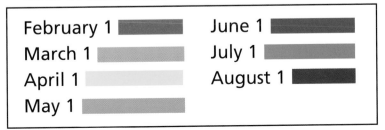

February 1
March 1
April 1
May 1
June 1
July 1
August 1

Plants & Pots

Once you've planned what plants you want to grow, you can buy them at a **nursery** or garden center. Directions that come with the seeds or **seedlings** will tell you how to plant them and when they will be **mature**.

The directions will also tell you if your plants are annuals or perennials. Annual plants grow for just one summer. Perennial plants grow in the summer, go **dormant** in the winter, and grow back again in the spring.

Once you've selected your plants, decide what kind of containers to put them in. Containers are usually made of wood, plastic, or **terra-cotta**.

Seed packets have useful information on the back side.

COSMOS

These early-blooming, daisy-like flowers will bloom until frost.

Plant Height	Plant Spacing	Planting Depth	Days to Germination
3-4 ft.	12-15 in.	1/4 in.	5-10

PLANTING INSTRUCTIONS
Plant in sunny location. Cosmos will grow in poor soil.

When to Plant Outdoors

	May-June
	April-June
	March-June
	Jan.-June
	Jan.-Dec.

10

This girl has chosen to plant her seedling in a plastic pot.

Preparing the Pots

Once you've picked out containers, it's time to get them ready for planting. The first step is to place a few rocks or a handful of gravel in the bottom of the container. This will help water drain from the pot.

Next, fill the container with potting soil. Fill it to about an inch or two (2.5 to 5 cm) from the top. Potting soil contains dirt, **peat moss**, and perlite.

Each part of the potting soil is important. Soil mixed with peat moss holds water for a longer time than regular dirt. Perlite looks like little, white balls. Perlite helps the soil drain excess water.

You can also mix a little **fertilizer** in with the potting soil. Fertilizer will make your plants grow bigger and help prevent disease.

A Pot Prepared for Planting

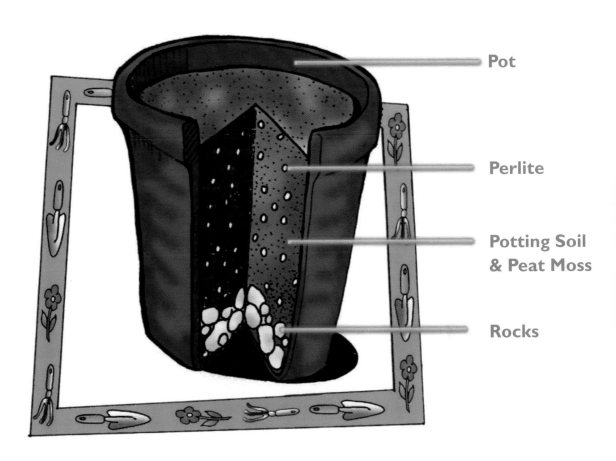

Pot

Perlite

Potting Soil
& Peat Moss

Rocks

Planting

Now that you have prepared the pots, it's time to plant. If you're planting seeds, the directions on the package will tell you how deep they need to be planted. Seeds can be planted in small pots first and then **transplanted** into large pots. Or, they can be planted directly into large pots.

If you're planting **seedlings**, dig a little hole in the soil and put the plant in. Make sure the base of the seedling is even with the top of the dirt. If it is planted too deep or too high, it will die.

Your new plants will go through many stages. The seeds will **germinate** and grow into seedlings. Seedlings will grow roots, stems, and leaves. Soon, buds will form and open into flowers. Then, birds and insects will **pollinate** the flowers and the process will begin again.

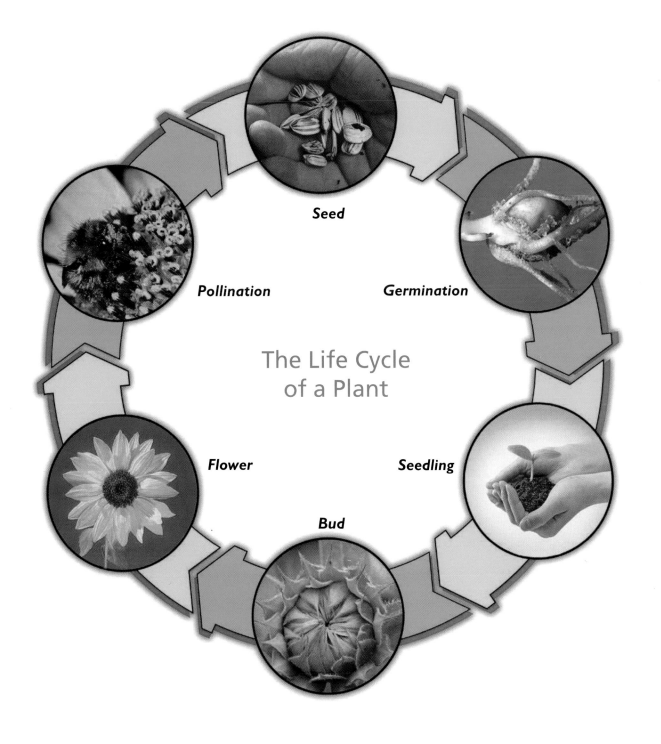

Seed

Germination

Pollination

The Life Cycle
of a Plant

Seedling

Flower

Bud

Watering

The best way to know if a plant needs water is to stick your finger into the soil. Does the soil feel dry and crumbly? If so, the plant needs water. Using a watering can is a good way to water a patio garden.

Pour enough water into the container so that it takes a minute or so for the water to soak into the soil. Plants that haven't been watered enough will turn brown and **wither**. Plants that have been watered too much will turn yellow and limp.

In the hottest days of summer, you might have to water every day. Other times of the year, watering two or three days a week will be fine. The only rule to watering is to check your plants and the soil every day.

Be careful not to dump water on newly planted seeds or seedlings.
Too much water could wash them out of their new homes.

Fertilizing

All plants need **nutrients** to grow. Soil has some nutrients in it already. Many gardeners add **fertilizer** to their soil. Fertilizer contains extra nutrients that help plants grow bigger and faster. Always ask an adult to help you apply fertilizer.

There are two main types of fertilizers, chemical and natural. Both types will provide your plants with extra nutrients to help them bloom.

Chemical fertilizers are available at garden centers. Some chemical fertilizers give plants a big burst of energy all at once. Others, called slow-release fertilizers, give plants the nutrients slowly over time.

Natural fertilizers are also available at garden centers. These fertilizers include manure and compost. Manure is a fertilizer made from animal waste. Compost is a fertilizer made from **decomposed** plant materials.

The nutrients in fertilizer help your plants grow healthy roots and leaves.

Maintenance

Watering and **fertilizing** aren't the only tasks gardeners do to keep their plants healthy. Weeding and pruning also help plants to grow their best. Luckily, patio gardens don't need much weeding. But pruning is still an important task.

If your plants are getting too tall, it's a good idea to prune them. This will make the plants fuller and bushier. It's also a good idea to remove any dead blossoms from your plants. This will make your plants look nicer. It will also encourage your flowers to bloom more often.

If you planted vegetables, they may require extra care. For example, vines like cucumbers, beans, and peas like to climb up posts. Putting a tall stick or post next to the base of the plant will help it grow well.

Pruning tools can be very sharp, so always ask an adult for help.

Garden Visitors

Another part of garden maintenance is inspecting the leaves and stems of your plants for harmful bugs. Are there big spots or little bugs crawling all over the stems and leaves? If so, call a garden center and ask for help. The professional gardeners there can tell you how to handle the problem.

Not all of the insects in your garden are harmful. Some actually help your garden to grow well. Bees and butterflies **pollinate** the flowers. Ladybugs eat other tiny insects that will hurt your plants.

Small animals, such as toads and birds, can also be helpful in your patio garden. Toads eat many grubs and insects that could harm your plants. Birds and bats also feast on bugs that are bad for your plants.

Certain insects such as ladybugs (top right), butterflies (center), and bees (lower right) help your garden stay healthy.

In the Fall

During the fall, it's time to clean up your garden and tools. If you clean your garden in the fall, you will be ready to plant right away next spring!

If you planted perennial flowers or herbs, you can save them for next spring. Just place the containers in a sunny window and remember to water them.

Vegetables and annuals cannot be saved for next year. Take the dead plants out of their containers and throw them away. It is also a good idea to empty the dirt from your containers and rinse them out well.

Cleaning your garden tools is also important in the fall. Removing the dirt from your tools will keep them from rusting.

Make sure to harvest all the fruits and vegetables before cleaning up your garden for the fall.

A Fun Project

Would you like to have a **unique** patio garden? Try using unusual containers. Almost anything will work if it can hold soil and won't fall apart when wet.

Be creative when you look for new containers. Do you have an old pair of shoes or boots that doesn't fit anymore? Fill them with potting soil and plant a marigold in each one. You could collect shoes from everyone you know and have a shoe garden!

Other household items work well as containers, too. Hats and baskets can be lined with plastic, filled with dirt, and planted with flowers. Old teapots or bird baths are great containers for small plants. Using interesting containers will make your patio garden both fun and unique.

*Be creative with your containers! This old wagon wheel
makes a great container for an herb garden.*

Plants to Start With

Most plants will grow in a container. Flowers, vegetables, and fruits are all great plants to start with. Below is a list of some of the easiest plants to grow.

Marigolds are annual flowers. They come in dark red, orange, yellow, and creamy white. Marigolds like full sun, and any soil.

Vegetables like tomatoes and pea pods grow well in sunny conditions. Tomatoes need lots of **fertilizer** to produce a good crop. Pea vines need posts to climb up.

Strawberries are an easy fruit for beginners to grow. They are perennials. They like full sun and well-drained soil. Garden centers sell special jars made just for growing strawberries.

Opposite page: Tomatoes (bottom), pea pods (left), and strawberries (right) are great plants for beginners.

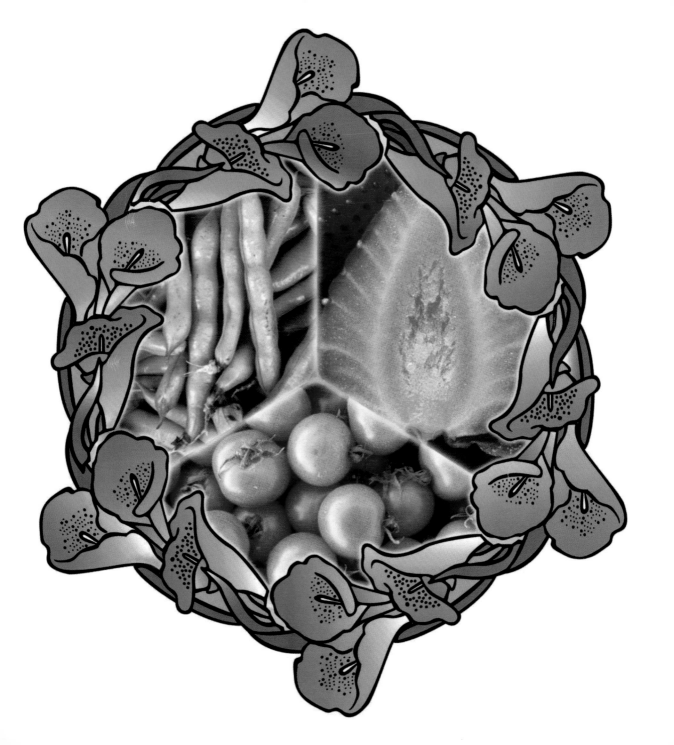

Glossary

decompose - to break down into simpler compounds.

dormant - a state of inactivity.

fertilizer - a substance used to help plants grow.

germinate - to sprout and begin to grow.

mature - a way to describe a plant that is fully grown.

nursery - a garden supply store and greenhouse where workers grow or sell plants.

nutrient - something naturally found in soil that helps plants grow.

peat moss - a pale green moss that grows in swamps and bogs.

pollinate - to transfer pollen by birds and insects from one flower or plant to another.

seedling - a young plant grown from seed.

terra-cotta - clay that has been heated to make it stronger.

transplant - to move a plant from one pot to another.

unique - being the only one of its kind.

wither - to become dry and lifeless.

Web Sites

The City Farmer
http://www.cityfarmer.org/
This site is sponsored by Canada's Office of Urban Agriculture. It has hundreds of links to information about gardening in small, urban spaces. Visitors will find information on everything from rooftop gardens to urban forestry.

Aggie Horticulture: Just for Kids
http://aggie-horticulture.tamu.edu/kindergarden/kinder.htm
This site is sponsored by the Horticulture Department at Texas A&M University. Visitors can view a slide presentation of children building a compost bin, learn why eating fresh fruits and vegetables is healthy, and discover many fun gardening projects.

These sites are subject to change. Go to your favorite search engine and type in Patio Gardens for more sites.

Index